PIANO • VOCAL • GUITAR

THE SONGS OF
IRVING BERLIN™
RAGTIME & EARLY SONGS

W9-CFK-105

Cover Photo: Irving Berlin seated at his desk in the offices of Waterson,
Berlin & Synder, Music Publishers, circa 1914.

ISBN 0-7935-0377-9

Hal Leonard Publishing Corporation
7777 West Bluemound Road P.O. Box 13819 Milwaukee, WI 53213

Photo Credit: Irving Berlin Archive

Irving Berlin with the chorus of the ZIEGFELD FOLLIES in the '20s.

THE SONGS OF
IRVING BERLIN™
RAGTIME & EARLY SONGS

CONTENTS

(LOOKING AT YOU)
ACROSS THE BREAKFAST TABLE

Words and Music by
IRVING BERLIN

Never saw such per-fect beau-ty be-

ALEXANDER'S RAGTIME BAND

Words and Music by
IRVING BERLIN

11

CRINOLINE DAYS

Words and Music by
IRVING BERLIN

EVERYBODY STEP

Words and Music by
IRVING BERLIN

EVERYBODY'S DOIN' IT NOW

Words and Music by
IRVING BERLIN

THE GIRL ON THE MAGAZINE COVER

Words and Music by
IRVING BERLIN

My head's in a diz-zy
My home is a pic-ture

if I could ev - er dis - cov - er, _____ A lit - tle

girl quite as nice as she. _____

_____ If I could meet, _____ a girl as

sweet, _____ I'd sim - ply claim her and

IF YOU DON'T WANT ME
(WHY DO YOU HANG AROUND)

Words and Music by
IRVING BERLIN

I'M GOING BACK TO THE FARM

Words and Music by
IRVING BERLIN

I'M ON MY WAY HOME

Words and Music by
IRVING BERLIN

I was blue ___ and mel-an-chol-y.
Not so sweet ___ are things that you chew,

44

LET ME SING AND I'M HAPPY

Words and Music by
IRVING BERLIN

NOBODY KNOWS
(AND NOBODY SEEMS TO CARE)

Words and Music by
IRVING BERLIN

MANDY

Words and Music by
IRVING BERLIN

MARIE

Words and Music by
IRVING BERLIN

AN ORANGE GROVE IN CALIFORNIA

Words and Music by
IRVING BERLIN

I've a long-ing to go, _____ Where the or-ang-es

SOMEONE ELSE MAY BE THERE
WHILE I'M GONE

Words and Music by
IRVING BERLIN

74

RUSSIAN LULLABY

Words and Music by
IRVING BERLIN

TELL ME LITTLE GYPSY

Words and Music by
IRVING BERLIN

THAT INTERNATIONAL RAG

Words and Music by
IRVING BERLIN

What did you do, A - mer - i - ca? They're af - ter you, A - mer - i - ca. You got ex - cit - ed and you start - ed some - thing,

strain _____ that they call __ the Span-ish Tan -

go. Dukes and lords and dip - lo - mats, _

dressed in tails and op - 'ra hats, _ throw up their

shoul - ders to that rag - ged - y mel - o - dy,

WHEN THE MIDNIGHT CHOO CHOO LEAVES FOR ALABAM'

Words and Music by
IRVING BERLIN

I've had a might-y bus-y day, _____ I've had to pack my things a - way. Now I'm goin' to give the